What's soft, cuddly, cute, and whimsical, yet functional?

My collection of 9 easy-to-crochet critters! Their sweet faces and winsome colors encourage imaginative playtime; the large size makes them perfect for nap time. Each animal has a special little "something" – embroidered facial details, braided tail, handy storage pocket, 3-D fish scales, you get the picture. Let's crochet your child's menagerie of fun!

contents ▾▾▾

LEISURE ARTS, INC. • Maumelle, Arkansas

SHOPPING LIST

Yarn (Medium Weight)

[3 ounces, 145 yards
(85 grams, 133 meters) per skein]:
☐ Brown - 3 skeins
[7 ounces, 370 yards
(198 grams, 338 meters) per skein]:
☐ Ecru - 75 yards (68.5 meters)

Crochet Hook

☐ Size H (5 mm)
or size needed for gauge

Additional Supplies

☐ 12 mm safety eyes - 2
☐ Yarn needle
☐ Polyester fiberfill

barry BEAR

◖■☐☐▷ **EASY**

Finished Size: 11" (28 cm) wide x 18" (45.5 cm) high

GAUGE INFORMATION

13 hdc and 9 rows = 4" (10 cm)
Gauge Swatch: 4" (10 cm) square
Ch 14.
Row 1: Hdc in third ch from hook (**2 skipped chs count as first hdc**) and in each ch across: 13 hdc.
Rows 2-9: Ch 2 (**counts as first hdc**), turn; hdc in next hdc and in each hdc across.
Finish off.

STITCH GUIDE

SINGLE CROCHET 2 TOGETHER (*abbreviated sc2tog*)
Pull up a loop in each of next 2 sc, YO and draw through all 3 loops on hook (**counts as one sc**).
HALF DOUBLE CROCHET 2 TOGETHER (*abbreviated hdc2tog*)
  (uses next 2 hdc)
★ YO, insert hook in **next** hdc, YO and pull up a loop; repeat from ★ once **more**, YO and draw through all 5 loops on hook (**counts as one hdc**).

BODY (Make 2)
With Brown, ch 26.

Row 1 (Right side): 2 Hdc in second ch from hook, hdc in next ch and in each ch across to last ch, 2 hdc in last ch: 27 hdc.

Note: Loop a short piece of yarn around any stitch to mark Row 1 as **right** side.

Rows 2-5: Ch 2 (**does not count as a st, now and throughout**), turn; 2 hdc in first hdc, hdc in next hdc and in each hdc across to last hdc, 2 hdc in last hdc: 35 hdc.

Rows 6-9: Ch 2, turn; hdc in first hdc and in each hdc across.

Row 10 (Decrease row): Turn; beginning in first hdc, hdc2tog, hdc in next hdc and in each hdc across to last 2 hdc, hdc2tog: 33 hdc.

Row 11: Ch 2, turn; hdc in first hdc and in each hdc across.

Rows 12 and 13: Repeat Rows 10 and 11: 31 hdc.

Rows 14 and 15 (Decrease rows): Turn; beginning in first hdc, hdc2tog, hdc in next hdc and in each hdc across to last 2 hdc, hdc2tog: 27 hdc.

Row 16: Ch 2, turn; hdc in first hdc and in each hdc across.

Rows 17-23: Repeat Rows 14-16 twice, then repeat Row 14 once **more**: 17 hdc.

Rows 24-28: Ch 2, turn; 2 hdc in first hdc, hdc in next hdc and in each hdc across to last hdc, 2 hdc in last hdc: 27 hdc.

Rows 29-33: Ch 2, turn; hdc in first hdc and in each hdc across.

Rows 34-36: Turn; beginning in first hdc, hdc2tog, hdc in next hdc and in each hdc across to last 2 hdc, hdc2tog: 21 hdc.

Row 37: Ch 2, turn; hdc in first hdc and in each hdc across.

Rows 38-41: Turn; beginning in first hdc, hdc2tog, hdc in next hdc and in each hdc across to last 2 hdc, hdc2tog; at end of Row 41, do **not** finish off: 13 hdc.

First Ear
Row 1: Do **not** turn; working in ends of rows, sc in first 5 rows, 2 sc in next row: 7 sc.

Rows 2 and 3: Ch 1, turn; sc in each sc across.

Row 4: Turn; beginning in first sc, sc2tog, sc in next 3 sc, sc2tog: 5 sc.

Row 5: Ch 1, turn; sc in each sc across.

Row 6: Turn; beginning in first sc, sc2tog, sc in next sc, sc2tog; finish off: 3 sc.

Second Ear
Row 1: With **right** side facing and working in ends of rows, join Brown with sc in Row 36 (**see Joining With Sc, page 45**); sc in same row and in last 5 rows: 7 sc.

Rows 2-6: Repeat Rows 2-6 of First Ear; at end of Row 6, do not finish off: 3 sc.

Trim
Ch 1, turn; sc in each sc; working in ends of rows, skip first row, sc in last 5 rows; sc in each hdc on Row 41; sc in first 5 rows on First Ear, skip last row; sc in each sc on Row 6 of First Ear; skip first row, sc in last 5 rows; work 41 sc evenly spaced across ends of rows of Body; sc in free loops of first 25 chs (**Fig. 3b, page 46**); work 41 sc evenly spaced across ends of rows of Body; sc in first 5 rows of Second Ear, skip last row; join with slip st to first sc, finish off: 146 sc.

POCKET

With Ecru, ch 20.

Row 1 (Right side): Sc in back ridge of second ch from hook and each ch across *(Fig. 1, page 46)*: 19 sc.

Note: Mark Row 1 as **right** side.

Row 2: Ch 1, turn; sc in each sc across.

Row 3: Ch 1, turn; slip st in each sc across.

Row 4: Ch 1, turn; working over slip sts on Row 3 and in sc on Row 2, sc in each sc across.

Rows 5-13: Ch 1, turn; sc in each sc across.

Row 14: Turn; beginning in first sc, sc2tog, sc in each sc across to last 2 sc, sc2tog: 17 sc.

Row 15: Ch 1, turn; sc in each sc across.

Rows 16-18: Turn; beginning in first sc, sc2tog, sc in each sc across to last 2 sc, sc2tog: 11 sc.

Finish off.

Trim: With **right** side facing, join Ecru with sc in end of Row 1; sc evenly across ends of rows to Row 18; sc in each sc across; sc evenly across ends of rows; finish off leaving a long end for sewing.

NOSE PATCH

Row 1 (Right side): With Ecru, ch 3, 2 sc in second ch from hook and in last ch: 4 sc.

Note: Mark Row 1 as **right** side.

Row 2: Ch 1, turn; 2 sc in first sc, sc in next 2 sc, 2 sc in last sc: 6 sc.

Rows 3-7: Ch 1, turn; sc in each sc across.

Row 8: Turn; beginning in first sc, sc2tog, sc in next 2 sc, sc2tog: 4 sc.

Row 9: Turn; beginning in first sc, sc2tog twice: 2 sc.

Trim: Ch 1, do **not** turn; sc evenly around entire piece; join with slip st to first sc, finish off leaving a long end for sewing.

FINISHING

Using photo as a guide for placement and with **right** sides facing:
• Attach eyes to front Body.
• With Taupe and using satin stitch *(Figs. 9a & b, page 47)*, add nose to Nose Patch.
• With Taupe and using backstitch, add mouth to Nose Patch *(Fig. 7, page 47)*.
• Using long ends, sew Nose Patch and Pocket to front Body.

Joining Rnd: With **wrong** sides together, working through **both** loops of each sc on **both** pieces, join Brown with slip st in any sc; slip st in each sc around stuffing Body firmly before closing; join with slip st to joining slip st, finish off.

SHOPPING LIST

Yarn (Medium Weight) 🔳4

[5 ounces, 256 yards
(141 grams, 234 meters) per skein]:
- ☐ White - 2 skeins
- ☐ Pink - 70 yards (64 meters)
- ☐ Orange - 30 yards
  (27.5 meters)
- ☐ Blue - 20 yards (18.5 meters)

Crochet Hook
- ☐ Size H (5 mm)
  or size needed for gauge

Additional Supplies
- ☐ 12 mm safety eyes - 2
- ☐ Yarn needle
- ☐ Polyester fiberfill

betty
BUNNY

EASY

Finished Size: 11½" (29 cm) wide x 22½" (57 cm) high

GAUGE INFORMATION

13 sc and 15 rows = 4" (10 cm)
Gauge Swatch: 4" (10 cm) square
Ch 14.
Row 1: Sc in second ch from hook and in each ch across: 13 sc.
Rows 2-15: Ch 1, turn; sc in each sc across.
Finish off.

STITCH GUIDE

TREBLE CROCHET (abbreviated tr)
YO twice, insert hook in ch indicated, YO and pull up a loop (4 loops on hook),
(YO and draw through 2 loops on hook) 3 times.
SINGLE CROCHET 2 TOGETHER (abbreviated sc2tog)
Pull up a loop in each of next 2 sc, YO and draw through all 3 loops on hook
(counts as one sc).

FRONT

With White, ch 28.

Row 1 (Right side): 2 Sc in second ch from hook, sc in each ch across to last ch, 2 sc in last ch: 29 sc.

Note: Loop a short piece of yarn around any stitch to mark Row 1 as **right** side.

Row 2: Ch 1, turn; 2 sc in first sc, sc in each sc across to last sc, 2 sc in last sc; finish off: 31 sc.

Row 3: With **right** side facing, join Pink with sc in first sc *(see Joining With Sc, page 45)*; sc in same st and in each sc across to last sc, 2 sc in last sc: 33 sc.

Row 4: Ch 1, turn; 2 sc in first sc, sc in each sc across to last sc, 2 sc in last sc; finish off: 35 sc.

Row 5: With **right** side facing, join Orange with sc in first sc; sc in same st and in each sc across to last sc, 2 sc in last sc: 37 sc.

Row 6: Ch 1, turn; sc in each sc across; finish off.

Row 7: With **right** side facing, join Blue with sc in first sc; sc in each sc across.

Row 8: Ch 1, turn; sc in each sc across; finish off.

Rows 9 and 10: With Orange, repeat Rows 7 and 8.

Rows 11 and 12: With Pink, repeat Rows 7 and 8.

Row 13: With **right** side facing, join White with sc in first sc; sc in each sc across.

Rows 14-20: Ch 1, turn; sc in each sc across.

Row 21 (Decrease row): Ch 1, turn; sc in first sc, sc2tog, sc in each sc across to last 3 sc, sc2tog, sc in last sc: 35 sc.

Row 22: Ch 1, turn; sc in each sc across.

Rows 23-32: Repeat Rows 21 and 22, 5 times: 25 sc.

Rows 33-36: Ch 1, turn; sc in first sc, sc2tog, sc in each sc across to last 3 sc, sc2tog, sc in last sc: 17 sc.

Rows 37-40: Ch 1, turn; sc in first sc, 2 sc in next sc, sc in each sc across to last 2 sc, 2 sc in next sc, sc in last sc: 25 sc.

Row 41: Ch 1, turn; sc in each sc across.

Row 42 (Increase row): Ch 1, turn; sc in first sc, 2 sc in next sc, sc in each sc across to last 2 sc, 2 sc in next sc, sc in last sc: 27 sc.

Rows 43-46: Repeat Rows 41 and 42 twice: 31 sc.

Rows 47-52: Ch 1, turn; sc in each sc across.

Row 53 (Decrease row): Ch 1, turn; sc in first sc, sc2tog, sc in each sc across to last 3 sc, sc2tog, sc in last sc: 29 sc.

Row 54: Ch 1, turn; sc in each sc across.

Rows 55-58: Repeat Rows 53 and 54 twice: 25 sc.

Rows 59-61: Ch 1, turn; sc in first sc, sc2tog, sc in each sc across to last 3 sc, sc2tog, sc in last sc: 19 sc.

Row 62: Ch 1, turn; sc in each sc across.

Rows 63-65: Ch 1, turn; sc in first sc, sc2tog, sc in each sc across to last 3 sc, sc2tog, sc in last sc: 13 sc.

Finish off.

First Ear

Row 1: With **right** side facing, skip first 8 sc on Row 65 and join White with sc in next sc; sc in last 4 sc and in end of next 4 rows: 9 sc.

Row 2: Ch 1, turn; 2 sc in first sc, sc in each sc across to last sc, 2 sc in last sc: 11 sc.

Rows 3 and 4: Ch 1, turn; sc in each sc across.

Finish off.

Row 5: With **right** side facing, join Pink with sc in first sc; sc in each sc across.

Row 6: Ch 1, turn; sc in each sc across; finish off.

Rows 7 and 8: With Orange, repeat Rows 5 and 6.

Rows 9 and 10: With Blue, repeat Rows 5 and 6.

Rows 11 and 12: With Orange, repeat Rows 5 and 6.

Rows 13 and 14: With Pink, repeat Rows 5 and 6.

Row 15: With **right** side facing, join White with sc in first sc; sc in each sc across.

Rows 16 and 17: Ch 1, turn; sc in first sc, sc2tog, sc in each sc across to last 3 sc, sc2tog, sc in last sc: 7 sc.

Row 18: Ch 1, turn; sc in first sc, (sc2tog, sc in next sc) twice: 5 sc.

Row 19: Turn; beginning in first sc, sc2tog, sc in next sc, sc2tog: 3 sc.

Row 20: Turn; beginning in first sc, sc2tog, beginning same st as last sc, sc2tog; finish off: 2 sc.

Second Ear

Row 1: With **right** side facing, join White with sc in end of Row 61; sc in end of next 3 rows and in first 5 sc on Row 65: 9 sc.

Rows 2-20: Work same as First Ear; at end of Row 20, do **not** finish off: 2 sc.

Trim

Ch 1, turn; sc in each sc and in end of each row across Second Ear; sc in each unworked sc on Row 65; sc in end of each row across First Ear and in each sc on Row 20; sc in end of each row across First Ear and across Front; sc in free loops of next 27 chs *(Fig. 3b, page 46)*; sc in end of each row across Front and across Second Ear; join with slip st to first sc, finish off: 244 sc.

BACK

With White, ch 28.

Row 1 (Right side)**:** 2 Sc in second ch from hook, sc in each ch across to last ch, 2 sc in last ch: 29 sc.

Note: Mark Row 1 as **right** side.

Rows 2-5: Ch 1, turn; 2 sc in first sc, sc in each sc across to last sc, 2 sc in last sc: 37 sc.

Rows 6-20: Ch 1, turn; sc in each sc across.

Rows 21-65: Work same as Rows 21-65 of Front; at end of Row 65, finish off: 13 sc.

First Ear

Row 1: With **right** side facing, skip first 8 sc on Row 65 and join White with sc in next sc; sc in last 4 sc and in end of next 4 rows: 9 sc.

Row 2: Ch 1, turn; 2 sc in first sc, sc in each sc across to last sc, 2 sc in last sc: 11 sc.

Rows 3-15: Ch 1, turn; sc in each sc across.

Rows 16 and 17: Ch 1, turn; sc in first sc, sc2tog, sc in each sc across to last 3 sc, sc2tog, sc in last sc: 7 sc.

Row 18: Ch 1, turn; sc in first sc, (sc2tog, sc in next sc) twice: 5 sc.

Row 19: Turn; beginning in first sc, sc2tog, sc in next sc, sc2tog: 3 sc.

Row 20: Turn; beginning in first sc, sc2tog, beginning same st as last sc, sc2tog; finish off: 2 sc.

Second Ear

Row 1: With **right** side facing, join White with sc in end of Row 61; sc in end of next 3 rows and in first 5 sc on Row 65: 9 sc.

Rows 2-20: Work same as Rows 2-20 of First Ear; at end of Row 20, do **not** finish off.

Trim

Ch 1, turn; sc in each sc and in end of each row across Second Ear; sc in each unworked sc on Row 65; sc in end of each row across First Ear and in each sc on Row 20; sc in end of each row across First Ear and across Back; sc in free loops of next 27 chs; sc in end of each row across Back and across Second Ear; join with slip st to first sc, finish off: 244 sc.

HEART

With Pink, ch 4, in fourth ch from hook work (2 tr, 3 dc, ch 1, tr, ch 1, 3 dc, 2 tr, ch 3, slip st); finish off leaving a long end for sewing.

FINISHING

Using photo, page 7, as a guide for placement and with **right** sides facing:

• Attach eyes to Front.

• Using long end, sew Heart to Front.

• With Blue and using satin stitch **(Figs. 9a & b, page 47)**, add nose to Front.

Joining Rnd: With **wrong** sides together, working through **both** loops of each sc on **both** pieces, join White with slip st in any sc; slip st in each sc around stuffing piece firmly before closing; join with slip st to joining slip st, finish off.

Tail

Make one 3" (7.5 cm) pom-pom **(Figs. A-C)**, using Blue, Orange, and Pink; then attach Tail to body.

making:
POM-POMS

Cut a piece of cardboard 3" (7.5 cm) square.

Wind the yarn around the cardboard until it is approximately ½" (12 mm) thick in the middle **(Fig. A)**. Carefully slip the yarn off the cardboard and firmly tie an 18" (45.5 cm) length of yarn around the middle **(Fig. B)**. Leave yarn ends long enough to attach the pom-pom. Cut the loops on both ends and trim the pom-pom into a smooth ball **(Fig. C)**.

Fig. A

Fig. B

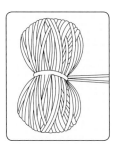

Fig. C

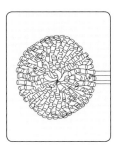

SHOPPING LIST

Yarn (Medium Weight)

[4.5 ounces, 247 yards
(127 grams, 225 meters) per skein]:
☐ Grey - 2 skeins
☐ Yellow - 25 yards (23 meters)
☐ White - 10 yards (9 meters)
☐ Blue - 10 yards (9 meters)

Crochet Hook
☐ Size H (5 mm)
   or size needed for gauge

Additional Supplies
☐ 12 mm safety eye
☐ Yarn needle
☐ Polyester fiberfill

ellis
ELEPHANT

◖◼◼☐☐ **EASY**

Finished Size: 16½" wide x 11½" high (42 cm x 29 cm)

GAUGE INFORMATION

13 sc and 15 rows = 4" (10 cm)
Gauge Swatch: 4" (10 cm) square
Ch 14.
Row 1: Sc in second ch from hook and in each ch across: 13 sc.
Rows 2-15: Ch 1, turn; sc in each sc across.
Finish off.

STITCH GUIDE

SINGLE CROCHET 2 TOGETHER *(abbreviated sc2tog)*
Pull up a loop in each of next 2 sc, YO and draw through all 3 loops on hook **(counts as one sc)**.
SINGLE CROCHET 3 TOGETHER *(abbreviated sc3tog)*
Pull up a loop in each of next 3 sc, YO and draw through all 4 loops on hook **(counts as one sc)**.

BODY (Make 2)

With Grey, ch 26.

Row 1: 2 Sc in second ch from hook, sc in each ch across to last 2 chs, 2 sc in each of last 2 chs: 28 sc.

Note: **For front Body,** loop a short piece of yarn around any stitch to mark Row 1 as **right** side; **for back Body,** loop a short piece of yarn around any stitch to mark Row 2 as **right** side.

Row 2 (Increase row): Ch 1, turn; 2 sc in first sc, sc in each sc across: 29 sc.

Row 3 (Increase row): Ch 1, turn; sc in each sc across to last sc, 2 sc in last sc: 30 sc.

Rows 4-11: Repeat Rows 2 and 3, 4 times: 38 sc.

Row 12 (Decrease row): Ch 1, turn; sc in each sc across to last 2 sc, sc2tog: 37 sc.

Row 13 (Decrease row): Turn; beginning in first sc, sc2tog, sc in each sc across: 36 sc.

Row 14: Ch 1, turn; sc in each sc across to last 5 sc, sc2tog, leave remaining 3 sc unworked: 32 sc.

Row 15: Repeat Row 13: 31 sc.

Row 16: Repeat Row 12: 30 sc.

Rows 17-24: Ch 1, turn; sc in each sc across.

Row 25: Ch 7, turn; 2 sc in second ch from hook, sc in each sc and in each sc across: 37 sc.

Rows 26-33: Ch 1, turn; sc in each sc across.

Row 34: Ch 1, turn; sc in each sc across to last 2 sc, sc2tog: 36 sc.

Row 35: Turn; beginning in first sc, sc2tog, sc in each sc across: 35 sc.

Row 36: Ch 1, turn; sc in each sc across to last 5 sc, sc2tog, leave remaining 3 sc unworked: 31 sc.

Row 37 (Decrease row): Turn; beginning in first sc, sc2tog, sc in each sc across: 30 sc.

Row 38 (Decrease row): Ch 1, turn; sc in each sc across to last 2 sc, sc2tog: 29 sc.

Rows 39-41: Repeat Rows 37 and 38 once, then repeat Row 37 once **more**: 26 sc.

Row 42: Ch 1 turn; sc in each sc across.

Row 43: Ch 6, turn; 2 sc in second ch from hook, sc in each ch and in each sc across: 32 sc.

Row 44: Turn; beginning in first sc, sc2tog, sc in each sc across to last sc, 2 sc in last sc.

Row 45 (Increase row): Ch 1, turn; 2 sc in first sc, sc in each sc across: 33 sc.

Rows 46 and 47: Repeat Rows 44 and 45: 34 sc.

Row 48: Turn; beginning in first sc, sc2tog, sc in each sc across: 33 sc.

Row 49: Ch 1, turn; sc in each sc across.

Row 50: Turn; beginning in first sc, sc2tog, sc in each sc across; do **not** finish off: 32 sc.

Trunk

Row 1 (Trunk begins): Ch 1, turn; sc in first 5 sc, sc2tog, leave remaining 25 sc unworked: 6 sc.

Rows 2-5: Ch 1, turn; sc in each sc across.

Row 6: Ch 6, turn; sc in second ch from hook and in each ch and each sc across: 11 sc.

Row 7 (Decrease row): Turn; beginning in first sc, sc2tog, sc in each sc across: 10 sc.

Row 8 (Decrease row): Ch 1, turn; sc in each sc across to last 2 sc, sc2tog: 9 sc.

Rows 9-12: Repeat Rows 7 and 8 twice; finish off: 5 sc.

Forehead

Row 1: On Row 50 of Body, skip next 5 unworked sc from Trunk and join Grey with slip st in next sc; beginning in same st, sc2tog, sc in each sc across to last 2 sc, sc2tog: 18 sc.

Row 2: Ch 1, turn; sc in each sc across to last 3 sc, sc3tog: 16 sc.

Row 3: Turn; beginning in first sc, sc2tog, sc in each sc across to last 2 sc, sc2tog: 14 sc.

Row 4: Ch 1, turn; sc in first 9 sc, sc2tog, leave remaining 3 sc unworked: 10 sc.

Row 5: Turn; beginning in first sc, sc2tog, sc in next 6 sc, sc2tog; do **not** finish off: 8 sc.

Trim

FRONT
Ch 1, do **not** turn; sc in end of next 65 rows across Forehead and across Body; sc in free loops of next 25 chs *(Fig. 3b, page 46)*; working in each sc, row and free loop of chs around legs, trunk, and Forehead, work 118 sc across; join with slip st to first sc: 208 sc.

BACK
Ch 1, turn; working in each sc, each row, and each free loops of chs around legs, trunk, and Forehead, work 110 sc across to beginning ch; sc in free loops of next 25 chs on Body; sc in end of next 65 rows across Body and across Forehead; sc in each sc on Row 5 of Forehead; join with slip st to first sc: 208 sc.

EAR

Row 1 (Right side)**:** With Blue, ch 3, sc in second ch from hook, 2 sc in last ch: 3 sc.

Note: Mark Row 1 as **right** side.

Row 2: Ch 1, turn; 2 sc in first sc, sc in last 2 sc; finish off: 4 sc.

Row 3 (Increase row)**:** With **right** side facing, join White with sc in first sc *(see Joining With Sc, page 45)*; sc in each sc across to last sc, 2 sc in last sc: 5 sc.

Row 4 (Increase row)**:** Ch 1, turn; 2 sc in first sc, sc in each sc across; finish off: 6 sc.

Rows 5 and 6: With Yellow, repeat Rows 3 and 4: 8 sc.

Row 7 and 8: Repeat Rows 3 and 4: 10 sc.

Row 9: With Blue, repeat Row 3: 11 sc.

Row 10: Ch 1, turn; sc in each sc across; finish off.

Row 11: Repeat Row 3: 12 sc.

Row 12: Ch 1, turn; sc in each sc across; finish off.

Row 13: With **right** side facing, join Yellow with sc in first sc; sc in each sc across.

Row 14: Ch 1, turn; sc in each sc across; finish off.

Rows 15 and 16: With White, repeat Rows 13 and 14.

Rows 17 and 18: With Blue, repeat Rows 13 and 14.

Rows 19-22: Repeat Rows 15-18.

Trim: With **right** side facing, join Yellow with sc in first sc on Row 22; sc in each sc across and in end of each row across; working in free loops of beginning ch, sc in next ch, 2 sc in next ch; sc in end of each row across and in same st as first sc; join with slip st to first sc, finish off leaving a long end for sewing.

FINISHING
Tail
Cut 3, 12" (30.5 cm) strands **each** of Grey, Blue **and** Yellow.
Knot one end and braid for 6" (15 cm). Knot and trim ends.

Using photo, page 13, as a guide for placement and with **right** side facing:
• Attach eye to front Body.
• Using long end, sew Ear to front Body.

Joining Rnd: With **wrong** sides together, working through **both** loops of each sc on **both** pieces, join Yellow with slip st in any sc; slip st in each sc around stuffing piece firmly before closing; join with slip st to joining slip st, finish off.

Attach Tail to Body.

elephant.

SHOPPING LIST

Yarn (Medium Weight)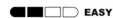

[4 ounces, 204 yards
(113 grams, 187 meters) per skein]:
- ☐ Variegated - 2 skeins

[5 ounces, 256 yards
(141 grams, 234 meters) per skein]:
- ☐ Pink - 1 skein

[4 ounces, 212 yards
(113 grams, 194 meters) per skein]:
- ☐ Grey - 1 skein

Crochet Hook
- ☐ Size H (5 mm)
  or size needed for gauge

Additional Supplies
- ☐ 12 mm safety eye
- ☐ Yarn needle
- ☐ Polyester fiberfill

fiona FISH

▓▓▓▓▢▢ **EASY**

Finished Size: 19" long x 10" high (48.5 cm x 25.5 cm)

GAUGE INFORMATION

13 sc and 15 rows = 4" (10 cm)

Gauge Swatch: 4" (10 cm) square

Ch 14.

Row 1: Sc in second ch from hook and in each ch across: 13 sc.

Rows 2-15: Ch 1, turn; sc in each sc across.

Finish off.

STITCH GUIDE

TREBLE CROCHET (abbreviated tr)

YO twice, insert hook in st indicated, YO and pull up a loop (4 loops on hook), (YO and draw through 2 loops on hook) 3 times.

SINGLE CROCHET 2 TOGETHER (abbreviated sc2tog)

Pull up a loop in each of next 2 sc, YO and draw through all 3 loops on hook **(counts as one sc)**.

SINGLE CROCHET 3 TOGETHER (abbreviated sc3tog)

Pull up a loop in each of next 3 sc, YO and draw through all 4 loops on hook **(counts as one sc)**.

FRONT
Body

With Variegated, ch 23.

Row 1 (Right side)**:** 2 Sc in second ch from hook, sc in each ch across to last ch, 2 sc in last ch: 24 sc.

Note: Loop a short piece of yarn around any stitch to mark Row 1 as **right** side.

Rows 2-5: Ch 1, turn; 2 sc in first sc, sc in each sc across to last sc, 2 sc in last sc: 32 sc.

Row 6: Ch 1, turn; 2 sc in first sc, sc in each sc across: 33 sc.

Row 7: Ch 1, turn; working in Front Loops Only *(Fig. 2, page 46)*, hdc in first sc, ★ skip next 3 sc, 7 dc in next sc, skip next 3 sc, hdc in next sc; repeat from ★ across.

Row 8: Ch 1, turn; working in free loops of Row 6 *(Fig. 3a, page 46)*, hdc in first hdc and in each sc across.

Row 9: Ch 3, turn; working in Front Loops Only, 3 dc in first hdc, skip next 3 hdc, hdc in next hdc, ★ skip next 3 hdc, 7 dc in next hdc, skip next 3 hdc, hdc in next hdc; repeat from ★ 2 times **more**, skip next 3 hdc, (3 dc, ch 3, slip st) in last hdc.

Row 10: Ch 1, turn; working in free loops of hdc one row **below** previous row, hdc in first hdc and in each hdc across.

Row 11: Ch 1, turn; working in Front Loops Only, hdc in first hdc, ★ skip next 3 hdc, 7 dc in next hdc, skip next 3 hdc, hdc in next hdc; repeat from ★ across.

Row 12: Ch 1, turn; working in free loops of hdc one row **below** previous row, hdc in each hdc across.

Rows 13-44: Repeat Rows 9-12, 8 times.

Row 45: Ch 1, turn; hdc in first hdc and in each hdc across; finish off.

Row 46: With **wrong** side facing, join Grey with sc in horizontal bar *(Fig. 5, page 46)* of first hdc *(see Joining With Sc, page 45)*; sc in horizontal bar of each hdc across.

Rows 47 and 48 (Decrease rows)**:** Turn; beginning in first sc, sc2tog, sc in each sc across to last 2 sc, sc2tog: 29 sc.

Row 49: Ch 1, turn; sc in each sc across.

Rows 50-55: Repeat Rows 47-49 twice: 21 sc.

Rows 56-60: Turn; beginning in first sc, sc2tog, sc in each sc across to last 2 sc, sc2tog: 11 sc.

Row 61: Ch 1, turn; sc in each sc across.

Row 62: Turn; beginning in first sc, sc2tog, sc in each sc across to last 2 sc, sc2tog: 9 sc.

Row 63: Turn; beginning in first sc, sc2tog twice, sc in next sc, sc2tog twice: 5 sc.

Row 64: Turn; beginning in first sc, sc2tog, sc in next sc, sc2tog: 3 sc.

Row 65: Turn; beginning in first sc, sc3tog; finish off.

Tail Fin
BASE

Row 1: With **right** side of Body facing and working free loops of beginning ch *(Fig. 3b, page 46)*, join Grey with sc in first ch; sc in same st, 2 sc in next ch, sc in next 18 chs, 2 sc in each of next 2 chs: 26 sc.

Rows 2-5: Ch 1, turn; 2 sc in first sc, sc in each sc across to last sc, 2 sc in last sc: 34 sc.

Rows 6 and 7: Ch 1, turn; sc in each sc across.

FIRST TIP

Row 1: Ch 1, turn; sc in first 13 sc, leave remaining 21 sc unworked.

Rows 2 and 3: Turn; beginning in first sc, sc2tog, sc in each sc across to last 2 sc, sc2tog; at end of Row 3, do **not** finish off: 9 sc.

SECOND TIP

Row 1: Do **not** turn; slip st in end of next 2 rows and in next 9 sc on Row 7 of Base, ch 1, sc in same st and in each sc across: 13 sc.

Rows 2 and 3: Turn; beginning in first sc, sc2tog, sc in each sc across to last 2 sc, sc2tog: 9 sc.

Finish off.

Trim

With **right** side facing, join Grey with sc in end of Row 1 of Base; sc in end of next 8 rows, skip last row; working across Row 3 of Second Tip, sc2tog, sc in next 5 sc, sc2tog; sc in end of next 2 rows, sc in next 11 slip sts; working across Row 3 of First Tip, sc2tog, sc in next 5 sc, sc2tog, skip first row, sc in end of next 9 rows changing to Pink in last sc made *(Fig. A, page 39)*; cut Grey, sc in end of each row across to last row of Variegated, sc in last row changing to Grey; cut Pink, sc in end of each row across; 3 sc in sc on Row 65; sc in end of each row across to last row of Grey, sc in last row changing to Pink in last sc; cut Grey, sc in end of each row across; join with slip st to first sc; finish off: 178 sc.

BACK
Body
With Pink, ch 23.

Rows 1-6: Work same as Front Body: 33 sc.

Rows 7-41: Ch 1, turn; sc in each sc across.

Rows 43-61: Work same as Rows 47-65 of Front Body.

Tail Fin
With Pink, work same as Front Tail Fin to Trim; do **not** finish off.

Trim: Ch 1, turn; sc2tog, sc in next 5 sc, sc2tog; sc in end of next 2 rows, sc in next 11 slip sts; working across Row 3 of First Tip, sc2tog, sc in next 5 sc, sc2tog; skip first row, sc in end of each row across; 3 sc in sc on Row 65; sc in end of each row across to last row, skip last row; join with slip st to first sc, finish off: 178 sc.

TOP FIN (Make 2)
With Grey, ch 21.

Row 1: Sc in second ch from hook and in each ch across: 20 sc.

Row 2: Ch 1, turn; sc in first 5 sc, hdc in next 5 sc, dc in next 5 sc, tr in last 5 sc.

Row 3: Ch 3, turn; tr in first 5 tr, dc in next 5 dc, hdc in next 5 hdc, sc in last 5 sc; finish off.

Joining Row: With pieces together, matching sts, and working through **both** thicknesses, join Grey with slip st in end of Row 3; slip st in each row across; working in free loops of beginning ch, slip st in each ch across; slip st evenly across ends of rows; slip st in each st across Row 3; join with slip st to joining slip st, finish off leaving a long end for sewing.

FINISHING
Using photo as guide for placement, attach eye to Front Body.

Joining Rnd: With **wrong** sides together, working through **both** loops of each sc on **both** pieces, join Pink with slip st in any sc; slip st in each sc around stuffing Body firmly before closing; join with slip st to joining slip st, finish off.

Using photo as a guide for placement and long end, sew Top Fin to top edge.

fish.

frank FOX

 **EASY**

Finished Size: 13" (33 cm) wide (excluding Tail) x 18" (45.5 cm) high

GAUGE INFORMATION

In pattern, (sc, ch 1, sc) 6 times and 11 rows = 4" (10 cm)
13 sc and 15 rows = 4" (10 cm)
Gauge Swatch: 4" (10 cm) square
Ch 12.
Work same as Body, page 22, for 11 rows: 6 ch-1 sps.
Finish off.

STITCH GUIDE

SINGLE CROCHET 2 TOGETHER *(abbreviated sc2tog)*
Pull up a loop in each of next 2 sc, YO and draw through all 3 loops on hook
(counts as one sc).

BODY (Make 2)

With Rust and beginning at side edge, ch 48.

Row 1 (Right side): (Sc, ch 1, sc) in second ch from hook, ★ skip next ch, (sc, ch 1, sc) in next ch; repeat from ★ across: 24 ch-1 sps.

Note: Loop a short piece of yarn around any stitch to mark Row 1 as **right** side.

Rows 2-36: Turn; (sc, ch 1, sc) in each ch-1 sp across: 48 sc and 24 ch-1 sps.

Trim: Ch 1, turn; 3 sc in first sc, skip next ch-1 sp, sc in next sc, ★ skip next sc, sc in next ch-1 sp and in next sc; repeat from ★ across to last ch-1 sp, skip next sc and last ch-1 sp, 3 sc in last sc; working in ends of rows, skip first row, sc in each row across to last row, skip last row; working in free loops of beginning ch (*Fig. 3b, page 46*), 3 sc in first ch, sc in each ch across to ch at base of last sc, 3 sc in ch; working in ends of rows, skip first row, sc in each row across to last row, skip last row; join with slip st to first sc, finish off: 170 sc.

BELLY

With White, ch 22.

Row 1 (Wrong side): Sc in second ch from hook and in each ch across: 21 sc.

Note: Mark the **back** of any stitch on Row 1 as **right** side.

Rows 2-20: Ch 1, turn; sc in each sc across.

Row 21 (Decrease row): Turn; beginning in first sc, sc2tog, sc in each sc across to last 2 sc, sc2tog: 19 sc.

Row 22: Ch 1, turn; sc in each sc across.

Rows 23-26: Repeat Rows 21 and 22 twice: 15 sc.

Rows 27-29: Turn; beginning in first sc, sc2tog, sc in each sc across to last 2 sc, sc2tog: 9 sc.

Trim: Ch 1, turn; sc in each sc across; sc in end of each row across; working in free loops of beginning ch, 3 sc in ch at base of first sc, sc in each ch across to last ch, 3 sc in last ch; sc in end of each row across; join with slip st to first sc, finish off leaving a long end for sewing.

FIRST EYE PATCH

With White, ch 13.

Row 1: Sc in second ch from hook and in each ch across to last ch, 2 sc in last ch: 13 sc.

Row 2 (Increase row): Ch 1, turn; 2 sc in first sc, sc in each sc across: 14 sc.

Row 3: Ch 1, turn; sc in each sc across.

Rows 4-7: Repeat Rows 2 and 3 twice: 16 sc.

Row 8: Ch 1, turn; 2 sc in first sc, sc in each sc across to last 2 sc, sc2tog.

Row 9: Ch 1, turn; sc in each sc across.

Row 10: Ch 1, turn; 2 sc in first sc, sc in each sc across to last 2 sc, sc2tog.

Row 11: Ch 1, turn; sc in first 12 sc, leave remaining 4 sc unworked.

Row 12: Ch 1, turn; 2 sc in first sc, sc in each sc across to last 2 sc, sc2tog.

Row 13: Ch 1, turn; sc in each sc across.

Rows 14-16: Repeat Rows 12 and 13 once, then repeat Row 12 once **more**.

Row 17: Turn; beginning in first sc, sc2tog, sc in next 9 sc, 2 sc in last sc.

Row 18: Ch 1, turn; 2 sc in first sc, sc in next 9 sc, sc2tog; do **not** finish off.

Trim (Right side): Ch 1, do **not** turn; sc in end of each row across to beginning ch; working in free loops of beginning ch, 3 sc in ch at base of first sc, sc in each ch across; sc in end of first 8 rows, skip next row, 3 sc in first sc on Row 10, sc in next 3 sc; sc in end of each row across; working across Row 18, 3 sc in first sc, sc in each sc across; join with slip st to first sc, finish off leaving a long for sewing.

Note: Mark Trim as **right** side.

SECOND EYE PATCH

Work same as First Eye Patch to Trim.

Trim (Right side): Ch 1, **turn**; sc in each sc across to last sc, 3 sc in last sc; skip first row, sc in end of next 8 rows; sc in first 3 unworked sc on Row 10, 3 sc in last sc; sc in end of each row across to beginning ch; working in free loops of beginning ch, sc in each ch across to ch at base of last sc, 3 sc in next ch; sc in end of each row across; join with slip st to first sc, finish off leaving a long for sewing.

Note: Mark Trim as **right** side.

EYE (Make 2)

Rnd 1 (Right side): With Black, ch 2, 5 sc in second ch from hook; do **not** join, place marker to indicate beginning of rnd *(see Markers, page 45)*.

Note: Mark Rnd 1 as **right** side.

Rnd 2: 2 Sc in each sc around; slip st in next sc, finish off: 10 sc.

Rnd 3: With **right** side facing, join White with sc in any sc *(see Joining With Sc, page 45)*; 2 sc in next sc, (sc in next sc, 2 sc in next sc) around; join with slip st to first sc, finish off leaving a long end for sewing.

With White, using photo as a guide for placement, and straight stitch *(Fig. 8, page 47)*, add accent to Eye.

NOSE

Rnd 1 (Right side): With Black, ch 2, 5 sc in second ch from hook; do **not** join, place marker to indicate beginning of rnd.

Note: Mark Rnd 1 as **right** side.

Rnd 2: 2 Sc in next sc, 2 hdc in next sc, sc in next sc, 2 hdc in next sc, 2 sc in next sc; slip st in next sc, finish off leaving a long end for sewing: 10 sts.

TAIL
First Side

Row 1: With White, ch 2, sc in second ch from hook: one sc.

Row 2 (Right side): Ch 1, turn; 2 sc in sc: 2 sc.

Note: Mark Row 2 as **right** side.

Row 3: Ch 1, turn; 2 sc in each of first 2 sc: 4 sc.

Row 4: Ch 1, turn; sc in each sc across.

Row 5 (Increase row): Ch 1, turn; 2 sc in first sc, sc in each sc across to last sc, 2 sc in last sc: 6 sc.

Row 6: Ch 1, turn; sc in each sc across.

Rows 7-12: Repeat Rows 5 and 6, 3 times: 12 sc.

Finish off.

Row 13: With **wrong** side facing, join Black with sc in first sc; sc in each sc across.

Rows 14 and 15: Ch 1, turn; sc in each sc across.

Finish off.

Row 16: With **right** side facing, join Rust with sc in first sc; sc in each sc across.

Rows 17-28: Ch 1, turn; sc in each sc across.

Row 29 (Decrease row): Turn; beginning in first sc, sc2tog, sc in each sc across: 11 sc.

Row 30: Ch 1, turn; sc in each sc across.

Rows 31-34: Repeat Rows 29 and 30 twice: 9 sc.

Rows 35 and 36: Turn; beginning in first sc, sc2tog, sc in each sc across to last 2 sc, sc2tog: 5 sc.

Row 37: Turn; beginning in first sc, sc2tog, sc in next sc, sc2tog: 3 sc.

Row 38: Turn; beginning in first sc, sc2tog, sc in last sc: 2 sc.

Trim: Ch 1, do **not** turn; sc in end of each row across to beginning ch; 3 sc in free loop of beginning ch; sc in end of each row across and in each sc on Row 38; join with slip st to first sc, finish off leaving a long end for sewing to Body: 81 sc.

Second Side

Rows 1-28: Work same as Rows 1-28 of First Side: 12 sc.

Row 29 (Decrease row): Ch 1, turn; sc in each sc across to last 2 sc, sc2tog: 11 sc.

Row 30: Ch 1, turn; sc in each sc across.

Rows 31-34: Repeat Rows 29 and 30 twice: 9 sc.

Rows 35 and 36: Turn; beginning in first sc, sc2tog, sc in each sc across to last 2 sc, sc2tog: 5 sc.

Row 37: Turn; beginning in first sc, sc2tog, sc in next sc, sc2tog: 3 sc.

Row 38: Turn; beginning in first sc, sc2tog, sc in last sc: 2 sc.

Trim: Ch 1, do **not** turn; sc in end of each row across to beginning ch; 3 sc in free loop of beginning ch; sc in end of each row across and in each sc on Row 38; join with slip st to first sc, finish off leaving a long end for sewing pieces together: 81 sc.

With **wrong** sides together, weave pieces together *(Fig. 6, page 46)* stuffing firmly before closing.

EAR (Make 4)

Row 1 (Right side): With Rust, ch 2, sc in second ch from hook: one sc.

Note: Mark Row 1 as **right** side.

Row 2: Ch 1, turn; 2 sc in sc: 2 sc.

Row 3: Ch 1, turn; 2 sc in each of first 2 sc: 4 sc.

Rows 4 and 5: Ch 1, turn; 2 sc in first sc, sc in each sc across to last sc, 2 sc in last sc: 8 sc.

Rows 6-10: Ch 1, turn; sc in each sc across.

Finish off.

Joining Rnd: With **wrong** sides of two Ears together and working through **both** layers, join Black with sc in end of Row 10; sc in end of each row across to beginning ch; 3 sc in free loop of beginning ch; sc in end of each row across; finish off leaving a long end for sewing.

Repeat with remaining two Ears.

FINISHING

Using photo as a guide for placement, with **right** sides facing and using long ends:

• Sew Eyes to Eye Patches.
• Sew Eye Patches, Nose, and Belly to front Body.
• Weave Body pieces together.
• Sew Tail and Ears to Body.

SHOPPING LIST
Yarn (Medium Weight)
[7 ounces, 370 yards
(198 grams, 338 meters) per skein]:
- ☐ Gold - 1 skein
- ☐ Brown - 1 skein

Crochet Hook
- ☐ Size H (5 mm)
  or size needed for gauge

Additional Supplies
- ☐ 12 mm safety eye
- ☐ Yarn needle
- ☐ Polyester fiberfill

george
GIRAFFE

EASY

Finished Size: 10" (25.5 cm) wide x 21" (53.5 cm) high

GAUGE INFORMATION
13 sc and 15 rows = 4" (10 cm)
Gauge Swatch: 4" (10 cm) square
Ch 14.
Row 1: Sc in second ch from hook and in each ch across: 13 sc.
Rows 2-15: Ch 1, turn; sc in each sc across.
Finish off.

STITCH GUIDE
SINGLE CROCHET 2 TOGETHER (abbreviated sc2tog)
Pull up a loop in each of next 2 sts, YO and draw through all 3 loops on hook **(counts as one sc)**.

FRONT

With Gold and beginning at top of head, ch 11.

Row 1 (Right side)**:** 2 Sc in second ch from hook and in next ch, sc in each ch across: 12 sc.

Note: Loop a short piece of yarn around any stitch to mark Row 1 as **right** side.

Row 2: Ch 1, turn; sc in each sc across to last 2 sc, 2 sc in each of last 2 sc: 14 sc.

Row 3 (Increase row)**:** Ch 1, turn; 2 sc in first sc, sc in each sc across: 15 sc.

Row 4: Ch 1, turn; sc in each sc across.

Rows 5-9: Repeat Rows 3 and 4 twice, then repeat Row 3 once **more**: 18 sc.

Row 10: Ch 1, turn; sc in each sc across to last sc, 2 sc in last sc: 19 sc.

Row 11: Ch 1, turn; 2 sc in first sc, sc in each sc across: 20 sc.

Row 12: Ch 1, turn; sc in each sc across to last sc, 2 sc in last sc: 21 sc.

Row 13: Turn; beginning in first sc, sc2tog, sc in each sc across: 20 sc.

Row 14: Ch 1, turn; sc in each sc across to last 2 sc, sc2tog: 19 sc.

Rows 15 and 16: Ch 1, turn; sc in each sc across; at end of Row 16, do **not** finish off.

Nose

Row 1: Ch 1, turn; sc in first 7 sc, sc2tog, leave remaining 10 sc unworked: 8 sc.

Row 2: Turn; beginning in first sc, sc2tog, sc in next 4 sc, sc2tog: 6 sc.

Row 3: Ch 1, turn; sc in first 4 sc, sc2tog: 5 sc.

Row 4: Turn; beginning in first sc, sc2tog, sc in next sc, sc2tog; finish off: 3 sc.

Neck & Body

Row 1: With **right** side facing, join Gold with sc in first unworked sc from Nose on Row 16 *(see Joining With Sc, page 45)*; sc in each sc across: 10 sc.

Rows 2-5: Ch 1, turn; sc in each sc across.

Row 6: Ch 1, turn; 2 sc in first sc, sc in each sc across: 11 sc.

Row 7 (Increase row)**:** Ch 1, turn; 2 sc in first sc, sc in each sc across to last sc, 2 sc in last sc: 13 sc.

Row 8: Ch 1, turn; sc in each sc across.

Rows 9-14: Repeat Rows 7 and 8, 3 times: 19 sc.

Row 15: Ch 1, turn; sc in each sc across to last sc, 2 sc in last sc: 20 sc.

Row 16: Ch 1, turn; 2 sc in first sc, sc in each sc across to last sc, 2 sc in last sc: 22 sc.

Row 17: Ch 1, turn; sc in each sc across to last sc, 2 sc in last sc: 23 sc.

Row 18: Ch 1, turn; 2 sc in each of first 2 sc, sc in each sc across: 25 sc.

Row 19: Ch 1, turn; 2 sc in first sc, sc in each sc across to last sc, 2 sc in last sc: 27 sc.

Row 20: Ch 1, turn; 2 sc in first sc, sc in each sc across: 28 sc.

Rows 21 and 22: Ch 1, turn; sc in each sc across to last sc, 2 sc in last sc: 30 sc.

Row 23: Ch 1, turn; sc in each sc across to last 2 sc, 2 sc in each of last 2 sc: 32 sc.

Row 24: Ch 1, turn; 2 sc in first sc, sc in each sc across: 33 sc.

Rows 25-41: Ch 1, turn; sc in each sc across.

Do **not** finish off.

First Leg

Row 1: Ch 1, turn; sc in first 12 sc, sc2tog, leave remaining 19 sc unworked: 13 sc.

Row 2: Turn; beginning in first sc, sc2tog, sc in each sc across: 12 sc.

Row 3: Ch 1, turn; sc in each sc across.

Row 4: Ch 1, turn; sc in each sc across to last 2 sc, sc2tog: 11 sc.

Rows 5-9: Ch 1, turn; sc in each sc across.

Row 10: Ch 1, turn; 2 sc in first sc, sc in each sc across to last 2 sc, sc2tog.

Row 11: Ch 1, turn; sc in each sc across.

Rows 12 and 13: Repeat Rows 10 and 11.

Finish off.

Row 14: With **right** side facing, join Brown with sc in first sc; sc in same st and in next 8 sc, sc2tog.

Rows 15-17: Ch 1, turn; sc in each sc across.

Row 18: Turn; beginning in first sc, sc2tog, sc in next 7 sc, sc2tog; finish off: 9 sc.

Second Leg

Row 1: With **wrong** side facing, skip next 5 sc from First Leg on Row 41 and join Gold with slip st in next sc; ch 1, beginning in same st as joining, sc2tog, sc in each sc across: 13 sc.

Row 2: Ch 1, turn; sc in each sc across to last 2 sc, sc2tog: 12 sc.

Row 3: Ch 1, turn; sc in each sc across.

Row 4: Turn; beginning in first sc, sc2tog, sc in each sc across: 11 sc.

Rows 5-9: Ch 1, turn; sc in each sc across.

Row 10: Turn; beginning in first sc, sc2tog, sc in each sc across to last sc, 2 sc in last sc.

Row 11: Ch 1, turn; sc in each sc across.

Rows 12 and 13: Repeat Rows 10 and 11.

Finish off.

Row 14: With **right** side facing, join Brown with slip st in first sc, beginning in same st as joining, sc2tog, sc in each sc across to last sc, 2 sc in last sc.

Rows 15-17: Ch 1, turn; sc in each sc across.

Row 18: Turn; beginning in first sc, sc2tog, sc in next 7 sc, sc2tog; finish off: 9 sc.

Horn

Row 1: With **right** side facing and working in free loops of beginning ch *(Fig. 3b, page 46)*, join Gold with sc in first ch; sc in next 3 chs: 4 sc.

Row 2: Turn; beginning in first sc, sc2tog, sc in last 2 sc: 3 sc.

Row 3: Ch 1, turn; sc in first sc, sc2tog; do **not** finish off: 2 sc.

Trim

Ch 1, do **not** turn; sc in end of next 3 rows; sc in free loops of next 6 chs; sc in end of next 20 rows; sc in next 3 sc on Row 4 of Nose; sc in end of next 59 rows; sc in first 9 chs on First Leg; sc in end of next 18 rows; sc in each 5 unworked sc on Row 41 of Body; sc in end of next 18 rows on Second Leg; sc in first 9 chs; sc in end of next 78 rows; sc in each sc on Row 3 of Horn; join with slip st to first sc, finish off: 230 sc.

BACK

With Brown and marking Row 2 as **right** side, work same as Front thru First Leg Row 13; do **not** finish off: 11 sc.

Row 14: Ch 1, turn; 2 sc in first sc, sc in each sc across to last 2 sc, sc2tog.

Rows 15-17: Ch 1, turn; sc in each sc across.

Row 18: Turn; beginning in first sc, sc2tog, sc in next 7 sc, sc2tog; finish off: 9 sc.

Second Leg

Row 1: With **right** side facing, skip next 5 sc from First Leg on Row 41 and join Brown with slip st in next sc; ch 1, beginning in same st as joining, sc2tog, sc in each sc across: 13 sc.

Rows 2-13: Work same as Front Second Leg; at end of Row 13, do **not** finish off.

Row 14: Turn; beginning in first sc, sc2tog, sc in each sc across to last sc, 2 sc in last sc.

Rows 15-17: Ch 1, turn; sc in each sc across.

Row 18: Turn; beginning in first sc, sc2tog, sc in next 7 sc, sc2tog; finish off: 9 sc.

Horn

Row 1: With **wrong** side facing and working in free loops of beginning ch, join Brown with sc in first ch; sc in next 3 chs: 4 sc.

Row 2: Turn; beginning in first sc, sc2tog, sc in last 2 sc: 3 sc.

Row 3: Ch 1, turn; sc in first sc, sc2tog: 2 sc.

Trim

Ch 1, turn; sc in each sc; sc in end of next 78 rows; sc in first 9 chs; sc in end of next 18 rows on Second Leg; sc in each 5 unworked sc on Row 41 of Body; sc in end of next 18 rows; sc in first 9 chs on First Leg; sc in end of next 59 rows; sc in next 3 sc on Row 4 of Nose; sc in end of next 20 rows; sc in free loops of next 6 chs; sc in end of last 3 rows; join with slip st to first sc, finish off: 230 sc.

SPOT #1 (Make 2)

With Brown, ch 4.

Row 1 (Right side): Sc in second ch from hook and in last 2 chs: 3 sc.

Note: Mark Row 1 as **right** side.

Row 2: Ch 3 (**counts as first dc, now and throughout**), turn; dc in first sc, 2 dc in next sc, leave last sc unworked: 4 dc.

Row 3: Ch 1, turn; sc in first 2 dc, sc2tog: 3 sc.

Row 4: Turn; beginning in first sc, sc2tog, beginning in same st as last sc, sc2tog; finish off leaving a long end for sewing.

SPOT #2 (Make 2)

Row 1 (Right side): With Brown, ch 4, 4 dc in fourth ch from hook (**3 skipped chs count as first dc**): 5 dc.

Note: Mark Row 1 as **right** side.

Row 2: Ch 3, turn; dc in first dc, 2 dc in next dc, leave remaining 3 dc unworked: 4 dc.

Row 3: Ch 1, turn; 2 sc in each of first 2 dc, leave remaining 2 dc unworked: 4 sc.

Row 4: Ch 1, turn; sc in each sc across.

Row 5: Turn; beginning in first sc, sc2tog twice; finish off leaving a long end for sewing.

SPOT #3 (Make 2)
With Brown, ch 4.

Row 1 (Right side)**:** Sc in second ch from hook and in last 2 chs: 3 sc.

Note: Mark Row 1 as **right** side.

Row 2: Ch 1, turn; sc in each sc across.

Row 3: Turn; beginning in first sc, sc2tog, beginning in same st as last sc, sc2tog; finish off leaving a long end for sewing.

SPOT #4
With Brown, ch 7.

Row 1 (Right side)**:** Sc in second ch from hook and in next 2 chs, dc in last 3 chs: 6 sts.

Note: Mark Row 1 as **right** side.

Row 2: Ch 3, turn; dc in first 2 dc, sc in next 3 sts, slip st in last sc: 7 sts.

Row 3: Turn; beginning in first slip st, sc2tog twice, dc in last 3 dc; finish off leaving a long end for sewing.

FINISHING
Tail
Cut 9 strands of Brown, **each** 12" (30.5 cm) long.
Knot one end and braid for 6" (15 cm).
Knot and trim end.

Using photo, page 30, as a guide for placement and with **right** sides facing:
• Attach eye to Front.
• Using long ends, sew Spots to Front.
• With Brown and using straight stitch *(Fig. 8, page 47)*, add mouth to Front.

Joining Rnd: With **wrong** sides together, working through **both** loops of each sc on **both** pieces, join Brown with slip st in any sc; slip st in each sc around stuffing Body firmly before closing; join with slip st to joining slip st, finish off.

Attach Tail to Body.

Mane
Cut 28, 3" (7.5 cm) strands of Brown.

Using photo as a guide for placement, working in sc *(Fig. A)* on Front Trim along back neck and beginning 2½" (6.25 cm) down from top of head, add fringe as follows:

Holding 2 strands together, fold in half. With Back facing and using crochet hook, draw folded end up through sc and pull the loose ends through the folded end *(Fig. B)*; draw the knot up tightly *(Fig. C)*. Repeat in next 13 sc.

Fig. A

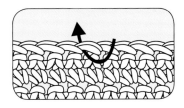

Fig. B   **Fig. C**

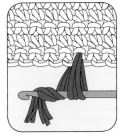 

larry LION

 **EASY**

Finished Size: 11½" (29 cm) wide x 15½" (39.5 cm) high

GAUGE INFORMATION

13 hdc and 9 rows = 4" (10 cm)

Gauge Swatch: 4" (10 cm) square

Ch 14.

Row 1: Hdc in third ch from hook (**2 skipped chs count as first hdc**) and in each ch across: 13 hdc.

Rows 2-9: Ch 2 (**counts as first hdc**), turn; hdc in next hdc and in each hdc across.

Finish off.

STITCH GUIDE

TREBLE CROCHET (*abbreviated tr*)

YO twice, insert hook in st indicated, YO and pull up a loop (4 loops on hook), (YO and draw through 2 loops on hook) 3 times.

SINGLE CROCHET 2 TOGETHER (*abbreviated sc2tog*)

Pull up a loop in each of next 2 sts, YO and draw through all 3 loops on hook (**counts as one sc**).

HALF DOUBLE CROCHET 2 TOGETHER (*abbreviated hdc2tog*)
  (uses next 2 sts)

★ YO, insert hook in **next** st, YO and pull up a loop; repeat from ★ once **more**, YO and draw through all 5 loops on hook (**counts as one hdc**).

HALF DOUBLE CROCHET 3 TOGETHER (*abbreviated hdc3tog*)
  (uses next 3 sts)

★ YO, insert hook in **next** st, YO and pull up a loop; repeat from ★ 2 times **more**, YO and draw through all 7 loops on hook (**counts as one hdc**).

BODY (Make 2)

With Tan, ch 27.

Row 1 (Wrong side)**:** 2 Hdc in second ch from hook and in each ch across to last ch, 2 hdc in last ch: 28 hdc.

Note: Loop a short piece of yarn around the **back** of any stitch on Row 1 to mark **right** side.

Row 2 (Increase row)**:** Ch 2 (**does not count as a st, now and throughout**), turn; working in Back Loops Only (*Fig. 2, page 46*), 2 hdc in first hdc, hdc in next hdc and in each hdc across to last hdc, 2 hdc in last hdc: 30 hdc.

Row 3 (Increase row)**:** Ch 2, turn; working in Front Loops Only (*Fig. 2, page 46*), 2 hdc in first hdc, hdc in next hdc and in each hdc across to last hdc, 2 hdc in last hdc: 32 hdc.

Rows 4-6: Repeat Rows 2 and 3 once, then repeat Row 2 once **more**: 38 hdc.

Row 7: Ch 2, turn; working in Front Loops Only, hdc in first hdc and in each hdc across.

Row 8: Ch 2, turn; working in Back Loops Only, hdc in first hdc and in each hdc across.

Rows 9-15: Repeat Rows 7 and 8, 3 times; then repeat Row 7 once **more**.

Row 16 (Decrease row)**:** Ch 2, turn; working in Back Loops Only, hdc in first hdc, hdc3tog, hdc in next hdc and in each hdc across to last 4 hdc, hdc3tog, hdc in last hdc: 34 hdc.

Row 17 (Decrease row)**:** Ch 2, turn; working in Front Loops Only, hdc in first hdc, hdc3tog, hdc in next hdc and in each hdc across to last 4 hdc, hdc3tog, hdc in last hdc: 30 hdc.

Rows 18 and 19: Repeat Rows 16 and 17: 22 hdc.

Place a marker in first and last hdc on Row 19 for Back Mane placement.

Row 20: Ch 2, turn; working in Back Loops Only, hdc in first hdc and in each hdc across, place a marker in first and last hdc for Mane placement.

Row 21 (Increase row)**:** Ch 2, turn; working in Front Loops Only, hdc in first hdc, 2 hdc in next hdc, hdc in next hdc and in each hdc across to last 2 hdc, 2 hdc in next hdc, hdc in last hdc: 24 hdc.

Row 22 (Increase row)**:** Ch 2, turn; working in Back Loops Only, hdc in first hdc, 2 hdc in next hdc, hdc in next hdc and in each hdc across to last 2 hdc, 2 hdc in next hdc, hdc in last hdc: 26 hdc.

Rows 23 and 24: Repeat Rows 21 and 22: 30 hdc.

Row 25: Ch 2, turn; working in Front Loops Only, hdc in first hdc and in each hdc across.

Row 26: Ch 2, turn; working in Back Loops Only, hdc in first hdc and in each hdc across.

Rows 27-31: Repeat Rows 25 and 26 twice, then repeat Row 25 once **more**.

Row 32 (Decrease row)**:** Ch 2, turn; working in Back Loops Only, hdc in first hdc, hdc3tog, hdc in next hdc and in each hdc across to last 4 hdc, hdc3tog, hdc in last hdc: 26 hdc.

Row 33 (Decrease row)**:** Ch 2, turn; working in Front Loops Only, hdc in first hdc, hdc3tog, hdc in next hdc and in each hdc across to last 4 hdc, hdc3tog, hdc in last hdc: 22 hdc.

Rows 34 and 35: Repeat Rows 32 and 33: 14 hdc.

Trim: Ch 1, turn; working in both loops, sc in each hdc across; work 54 sc evenly spaced across ends of rows; sc in free loops of next 26 chs (*Fig. 3b, page 46*); work 54 sc evenly spaced across ends of rows; join with slip st to first sc, finish off: 167 sc.

EAR (Make 2)

Row 1: With Tan, ch 2, sc in second ch from hook: one sc.

Row 2 (Right side): Ch 1, turn; 2 sc in sc: 2 sc.

Note: Mark Row 2 as **right** side.

Row 3: Ch 1, turn; 2 sc in each of first 2 sc: 4 sc.

Row 4: Ch 1, turn; 2 sc in first sc, sc in next 2 sc, 2 sc in last sc: 6 sc.

Rows 5-7: Ch 1, turn; sc in each sc across.

Row 8: Turn; beginning in first sc, sc2tog, sc in next 2 sc, sc2tog: 4 sc.

Trim: Ch 1, do **not** turn; sc in end of each row across to beginning ch; 3 sc in free loop of beginning ch, sc in end of each row across; finish off leaving a long end for sewing.

TAIL

With Taupe, ch 37.

Row 1 (Right side): Working in back ridge of beginning ch *(Fig. 1, page 46)*, dc in fourth ch from hook and in each ch across to last 2 chs, sc in last 2 chs.

Note: Mark Row 1 as **right** side.

Tuft

Rnd 1: Ch 10, sc in second ch from hook, hdc in next ch, 2 dc in next ch, tr in next 2 chs, 2 dc in next ch, hdc in next ch, sc in next ch, slip st in last ch; working in free loops on opposite side of ch-10, sc in next ch, hdc in next ch, 2 dc in next ch, tr in next 2 chs, 2 dc in next ch, hdc in next ch, sc in next ch; join with slip st to first sc, finish off leaving a long end for sewing.

FINISHING

Using photo as a guide for placement and with **right** sides facing:
- Attach eyes to front Body.
- With Taupe and using satin stitch *(Figs. 9a & b, page 47)*, add nose to front.
- With Taupe and using straight stitch *(Fig. 8, page 47)*, add mouth to front.

Joining Rnd: With **wrong** sides together and front facing, working through **both** loops of each sc on **both** pieces, join Blue with slip st in any sc; slip st in each sc around stuffing Body firmly before closing; join with slip st to joining slip st, finish off.

Using long end, sew Tail to Body.

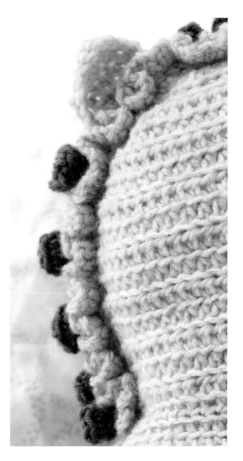

Mane

BACK

Row 1: With **right** side of front facing and working in sc on Back Trim, join Taupe with sc in sc at end of marked row; remove marker, sc in each sc across to next marked row, remove marker.

Row 2: Ch 2, turn; 2 dc in first sc and in each sc across.

Row 3: Ch 1, turn; (sc, ch 1, sc) in each dc across; finish off.

FRONT

Row 1: With **right** side of front facing and working in sc on Front Trim, join Blue with sc in sc at end of marked row; remove marker, sc in same st, 2 sc in each sc across to next marked row, remove marker.

Row 2: Ch 1, turn; (sc, ch 1, sc) in each sc across; finish off.

Using photo as a guide for placement and long ends, sew Ears to Body between Back and Front Mane.

SHOPPING LIST
Yarn (Medium Weight)
[4.5 ounces, 247 yards
(127 grams, 225 meters) per skein]:
- ☐ Blue - 2 skeins
- ☐ Ecru - 1 skein
- ☐ Pink - 25 yards (23 meters)
- ☐ Light Pink - 15 yards
  (13.5 meters)
- ☐ Peach - small amount
- ☐ Black - small amount

Crochet Hook
- ☐ Size H (5 mm)
  or size needed for gauge

Additional Supplies
- ☐ Yarn needle
- ☐ Polyester fiberfill

olivia
OWL

◖■■☐☐◗ **EASY**

Finished Size: 10½" (26.5 cm) wide x 14½" (37 cm) high

GAUGE INFORMATION
13 sc and 15 rows = 4" (10 cm)
Gauge Swatch: 4" (10 cm) square
Ch 14.
Row 1: Sc in second ch from hook and in each ch across: 13 sc.
Rows 2-15: Ch 1, turn; sc in each sc across.
Finish off.

STITCH GUIDE
SINGLE CROCHET 2 TOGETHER (abbreviated sc2tog)
Pull up a loop in each of next 2 sc, YO and draw through all 3 loops on hook
(counts as one sc).
FRONT POST DOUBLE CROCHET (abbreviated FPdc)
YO, insert hook from **front** to **back** around post of st indicated (**Fig. 4, page 46**),
YO and pull up a loop (3 loops on hook), (YO and draw through 2 loops on
hook) twice.
BACK POST DOUBLE CROCHET (abbreviated BPdc)
YO, insert hook from **back** to **front** around post of st indicated (**Fig. 4, page 46**),
YO and pull up a loop (3 loops on hook), (YO and draw through 2 loops on
hook) twice.

BODY (Make 2)

With Blue, ch 31.

Row 1 (Right side): 2 Sc in second ch from hook, sc in each ch across to last ch, 2 sc in last ch: 32 sc.

Note: Loop a short piece of yarn around any stitch to mark Row 1 as **right** side.

Row 2: Ch 1, turn; 2 sc in first sc, sc in each sc across to last sc, 2 sc in last sc: 34 sc.

Rows 3-40: Ch 1, turn; sc in each sc across.

Row 41 (Decrease row): Turn; beginning in first sc, sc2tog, sc in each sc across to last 2 sc, sc2tog: 32 sc.

Row 42: Ch 1, turn; sc in each sc across.

Rows 43-55: Repeat Rows 41 and 42, 6 times; then repeat Row 41 once **more**: 18 sc.

Trim: Ch 1, do **not** turn; sc in end of each row across; sc in free loops of next 30 chs *(Fig. 3b, page 46)*; sc in end of each row across; sc in each sc across Row 55; join with slip st to first sc, finish off: 158 sc.

MASK

With Ecru, ch 7.

Row 1 (Wrong side): 2 Sc in second ch from hook, sc in each ch across to last ch, 2 sc in last ch: 8 sc.

Note: Mark the **back** of any stitch on Row 1 as **right** side.

Rows 2 and 3: Ch 1, turn; 2 sc in first sc, sc in each sc across to last sc, 2 sc in last sc: 12 sc.

Row 4: Ch 1, turn; sc in each sc across.

Row 5 (Increase row): Ch 1, turn; sc in each sc across to last sc, 2 sc in last sc: 13 sc.

Rows 6 and 7: Repeat Rows 4 and 5: 14 sc.

Rows 8-12: Ch 1, turn; sc in each sc across.

Row 13: Ch 1, turn; sc in each sc across to last 2 sc, sc2tog: 13 sc.

Row 14: Ch 1, turn; sc in each sc across.

Row 15: Ch 1, turn; sc in each sc across to last 2 sc, sc2tog: 12 sc.

Row 16: Turn; beginning in first sc, sc2tog, sc in each sc across: 11 sc.

Row 17: Ch 1, turn; sc in each sc across to last sc, 2 sc in last sc: 12 sc.

Row 18: Ch 1, turn; sc in each sc across.

Row 19: Ch 1, turn; sc in each sc across to last sc, 2 sc in last sc: 13 sc.

Row 20: Ch 1, turn; 2 sc in first sc, sc in each sc across: 14 sc.

Rows 21-25: Ch 1, turn; sc in each sc across.

Row 26 (Decrease row): Turn; beginning in first sc, sc2tog, sc in each sc across: 13 sc.

Row 27: Ch 1, turn; sc in each sc across.

Rows 28 and 29: Repeat Rows 26 and 27: 12 sc.

Rows 30-32: Turn; beginning in first sc, sc2tog, sc in each sc across to last 2 sc, sc2tog: 6 sc.

Trim: Ch 1, do **not** turn; sc in end of each row across; working in free loops of beginning ch, sc in ch at base of first sc and in each ch across; sc in end of each row across and in each sc across Row 32; join with slip st to first sc, finish off leaving a long end for sewing.

Eyes: With Black and using photo, page 37, as a guide for placement, add eyes to Mask, using backstitch *(Fig. 7, page 47)* and straight stitch *(Fig. 8, page 47)*.

Beak: With Peach and using photo as a guide for placement, add beak to Mask, using satin stitch *(Figs. 9a & b, page 47)*.

WING (Make 2)

Row 1 (Right side): With Ecru, ch 2, sc in second ch from hook: one sc.

Note: Mark Row 1 as **right** side.

Row 2: Ch 1, turn; 2 sc in sc: 2 sc.

Row 3: Ch 1, turn; 2 sc in each of first 2 sc: 4 sc.

Rows 4-6: Ch 1, turn; sc in each sc across.

Row 7: Ch 1, turn; 2 sc in first sc, sc in next 2 sc, 2 sc in last sc: 6 sc.

Rows 8-14: Ch 1, turn; sc in each sc across.

owl.

Row 15: Turn; beginning in first sc, sc2tog, sc in next 2 sc, sc2tog: 4 sc.

Rows 16-18: Ch 1, turn; sc in each sc across.

Row 19: Turn; beginning in first sc, sc2tog twice: 2 sc.

Row 20: Ch 1, turn; sc in each sc across.

Row 21: Turn; beginning in first sc, sc2tog: one sc.

Trim: Ch 1, do **not** turn; sc in end of each row across; sc in free loop of ch at base of first sc; sc in end of each row across, sc in sc on Row 21; join with slip st to first sc, finish off leaving a long end for sewing.

POCKET
With Light Pink, ch 13.

Row 1 (Right side): 2 Sc in second ch from hook, sc in each ch across to last sc, 2 sc in last ch: 14 sc.

Note: Mark Row 1 as **right** side.

Row 2: Ch 1, turn; 2 sc in first sc, sc in each sc across to last sc, 2 sc in last sc changing to Pink in last sc *(Fig. A)*; drop Light Pink: 16 sc.

Fig. A

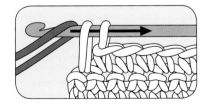

Carry unused yarn loosely along edge.

Row 3: Ch 1, turn; 2 sc in first sc, sc in each sc across to last sc, 2 sc in last sc: 18 sc.

Row 4: Ch 1, turn; sc in each sc across changing to Light Pink in last sc; drop Pink.

Row 5: Ch 1, turn; sc in each sc across.

Row 6: Ch 1, turn; sc in each sc across changing to Pink in last sc; drop Light Pink.

Rows 7 and 8: Repeat Rows 5 and 6; at end of Row 8, change to Light Pink; drop Pink.

Rows 9-17: Repeat Rows 5-8 twice, then repeat Row 5 once **more**.

Row 18: Ch 1, turn; sc in each sc across changing to Pink in last sc; cut Light Pink.

Row 19: Ch 2 (**does not count as a st, now and throughout**), turn; dc in first sc and in each sc across.

Rows 20 and 21: Ch 2, turn; dc in first dc, (work FPdc around next st, work BPdc around next st) across to last dc, dc in last dc.

Trim: Ch 1, do **not** turn; sc evenly across ends of rows; sc in free loops of next 12 chs; sc evenly across ends of rows; finish off leaving a long end for sewing.

FINISHING
Using photo as a guide for placement, with **right** sides facing and using long ends, sew Eye Mask, Pocket, and Wings to front Body.

Tufts
Cut 4, 5" (12.5 cm) strands **each** of Pink and Light Pink. Holding 2 strands each of Pink and Light Pink together, add fringe to each top corner on Body *(Figs. A-C, page 31)*. Trim ends evenly.

Joining Rnd: With **wrong** sides together, working through **both** loops of each sc on **both** pieces, join Blue with slip st in any sc; slip st in each sc around stuffing Body firmly before closing; join with slip st to joining slip st, finish off.

penny
PENGUIN

EASY

Finished Size: 11½" (29 cm) wide x 17½" (44.5 cm) high

GAUGE INFORMATION

13 sc and 15 rows = 4" (10 cm)
Gauge Swatch: 4" (10 cm) square
Ch 14.
Row 1: Sc in second ch from hook and in each ch across: 13 sc.
Rows 2-15: Ch 1, turn; sc in each sc across.
Finish off.

STITCH GUIDE

SINGLE CROCHET 2 TOGETHER (abbreviated sc2tog)
Pull up a loop in each of next 2 sts, YO and draw through all 3 loops on hook **(counts as one sc)**.

HALF DOUBLE CROCHET 2 TOGETHER (abbreviated hdc2tog)
 (uses next 2 sts)
★ YO, insert hook in **next** st, YO and pull up a loop; repeat from ★ once **more**, YO and draw through all 5 loops on hook **(counts as one hdc)**.

BODY (Make 2)
With Black, ch 26.

Row 1 (Wrong side)**:** 2 Sc in first ch, sc in each ch across to last ch, 2 sc in last ch: 27 sc.

Note: Loop a short piece of yarn around the **back** of any stitch on Row 1 to mark **right** side.

Rows 2-6: Ch 1, turn; 2 sc in first sc, sc in each sc across to last sc, 2 sc in last sc: 37 sc.

Rows 7-30: Ch 1, turn; sc in each sc across.

Row 31 (Decrease row)**:** Turn; beginning in first sc, sc2tog, sc in each sc across to last 2 sc, sc2tog: 35 sc.

Rows 32-35: Ch 1, turn; sc in each sc across.

Rows 36-55: Repeat Rows 31-35, 4 times: 27 sc.

Row 56 (Decrease row)**:** Turn; beginning in first sc, sc2tog, sc in each sc across to last 2 sc, sc2tog: 25 sc.

Row 57: Ch 1, turn; sc in each sc across.

Rows 58 and 59: Repeat Rows 56 and 57: 23 sc.

Rows 60-62: Repeat Row 56, 3 times: 17 sc.

Row 63: Ch 1, turn; sc in each sc across.

Row 64: Repeat Row 56: 15 sc.

Trim: Ch 1, do **not** turn; sc in end of each row across; working in free loops of beginning ch, sc in ch at base of first sc and in next 24 chs *(Fig. 3b, page 46)*; sc in end of each row across and in each sc across Row 64; join with slip st to first sc, finish off: 168 sc.

FRONT
With White, ch 19.

Row 1 (Right side)**:** 2 Sc in second ch from hook, sc in each ch across to last ch, 2 sc in last ch: 20 sc.

Note: Mark Row 1 as **right** side.

Rows 2-7: Ch 1, turn; 2 sc in first sc, sc in each sc across to last sc, 2 sc in last sc: 32 sc.

Rows 8-20: Ch 1, turn; sc in each sc across.

Row 21 (Decrease row)**:** Turn; beginning in first sc, sc2tog, sc in each sc across to last 2 sc, sc2tog: 30 sc.

Row 22: Ch 1, turn; sc in each sc across.

Rows 23-33: Repeat Rows 21 and 22, 5 times; then repeat Row 21 once **more**: 18 sc.

Rows 34-37: Ch 1, turn; sc in each sc across.

Row 38 (Increase row)**:** Ch 1, turn; 2 sc in first sc, sc in each sc across to last sc, 2 sc in last sc: 20 sc.

Rows 39 and 40: Ch 1, turn; sc in each sc across.

Rows 41-45: Repeat Rows 38-40 once, then repeat Rows 38 and 39 once **more**: 24 sc.

Row 46 (Decrease row)**:** Turn; beginning in first sc, sc2tog, sc in each sc across to last 2 sc, sc2tog: 22 sc.

Row 47: Ch 1, turn; sc in each sc across.

Rows 48 and 49: Repeat Rows 46 and 47: 20 sc.

First Shaping
Row 1: Turn; beginning in first sc, sc2tog, sc in next 6 sc, sc2tog, leave remaining 10 sc unworked: 8 sc.

Row 2: Ch 1, turn; sc in each sc across.

Row 3: Turn; beginning in first sc, sc2tog, sc in next 4 sc, sc2tog: 6 sc.

Row 4: Turn; beginning in first sc, sc2tog, sc in next 2 sc, sc2tog; finish off: 4 sc.

Second Shaping

Row 1: With **wrong** side facing, join White with slip st in first unworked sc from First Shaping; beginning in same st, sc2tog, sc in next 6 sc, sc2tog: 8 sc.

Rows 2-4: Repeat Rows 2-4 of First Shaping; at end of Row 4; at end of Row 4, do **not** finish off.

Trim

Ch 1, do **not** turn; sc in end of next 3 rows, (sc in same sc on Row 49 as next sc) twice; sc in end of next 3 rows; sc in next 4 sc of First Side Shaping; sc in end of each row across and in free loops of next 18 chs; sc in end of each row across and in next 4 sc of Second Side Shaping; join with slip st to first sc, finish off leaving a long end for sewing.

POCKET

With Orange and beginning at top edge, ch 20.

Row 1 (Right side): Sc in back ridge of second ch from hook and each ch across *(Fig. 1, page 46)*: 19 sc.

Note: Mark Row 1 as **right** side.

Rows 2-4: Ch 1, turn; sc in each sc across.

Row 5: Ch 2 **(does not count as a st, now and throughout)**, turn; hdc in first sc and in each sc across.

Row 6: Ch 1, turn; sc in horizontal bar of each hdc across *(Fig. 5, page 46)*.

Rows 7-15: Repeat Rows 5 and 6, 4 times; then repeat Row 5 once **more**.

Row 16 (Decrease row): Ch 1, turn; working in horizontal bar of hdc and beginning in first hdc, sc2tog twice, sc in each hdc across to last 4 hdc, sc2tog twice: 15 sc.

Row 17: Turn; beginning in first sc, hdc2tog, hdc in next sc and in each sc across to last 2 sc, hdc2tog: 13 hdc.

Row 18: Repeat Row 16; finish off: 11 sc.

Trim: With **right** side facing, join Orange with sc in end of Row 1; sc evenly across ends of rows and in each sc across Row 18; sc evenly across ends of rows; finish off leaving a long end for sewing.

FINISHING

Using photo, page 41, as a guide for placement, with **right** side facing and using long ends:
- Sew Pocket to Front.
- Using satin stitch *(Figs. 9a & b, page 47)*, add Orange beak to Front.
- Sew Front to one Body.
- Attach eyes to Front.

With **wrong** sides together, weave Body pieces together *(Fig. 6, page 46)* stuffing firmly before closing.

GENERAL INSTRUCTIONS

ABBREVIATIONS

BPdc	Back Post double crochet(s)
ch(s)	chain(s)
cm	centimeters
dc	double crochet(s)
FPdc	Front Post double crochet(s)
hdc	half double crochet(s)
hdc2tog	half double crochet 2 together
hdc3tog	half double crochet 3 together
mm	millimeters
Rnd(s)	Round(s)
sc	single crochet(s)
sc2tog	single crochet 2 together
sc3tog	single crochet 3 together
sp(s)	space(s)
st(s)	stitch(es)
tr	treble crochet(s)
YO	yarn over

SYMBOLS & TERMS

★ — work instructions following ★ as many **more** times as indicated in addition to the first time.

( ) or [ ] — work enclosed instructions **as many** times as specified by the number immediately following **or** work all enclosed instructions in the stitch or space indicated **or** contains explanatory remarks.

colon (:) — the number(s) given after a colon at the end of a row or round denote(s) the number of stitches or spaces you should have on that row or round.

Yarn Weight Symbol & Names	LACE 0	SUPER FINE 1	FINE 2	LIGHT 3	MEDIUM 4	BULKY 5	SUPER BULKY 6	JUMBO 7
Type of Yarns in Category	Fingering, size 10 crochet thread	Sock, Fingering, Baby	Sport, Baby	DK, Light Worsted	Worsted, Afghan, Aran	Chunky, Craft, Rug	Super Bulky, Roving	Jumbo, Roving
Crochet Gauge* Ranges in Single Crochet to 4" (10 cm)	32-42 sts**	21-32 sts	16-20 sts	12-17 sts	11-14 sts	8-11 sts	6-9 sts	5 sts and fewer
Advised Hook Size Range	Steel*** 6 to 8, Regular hook B-1	B-1 to E-4	E-4 to 7	7 to I-9	I-9 to K-10½	K-10½ to M/N-13	M/N-13 to Q	Q and larger

*GUIDELINES ONLY: The chart above reflects the most commonly used gauges and hook sizes for specific yarn categories.

** Lace weight yarns are usually crocheted with larger hooks to create lacy openwork patterns. Accordingly, a gauge range is difficult to determine. Always follow the gauge stated in your pattern.

*** Steel crochet hooks are sized differently from regular hooks–the higher the number, the smaller the hook, which is the reverse of regular hook sizing.

CROCHET HOOKS

U.S.	Metric mm
B-1	2.25
C-2	2.75
D-3	3.25
E-4	3.5
F-5	3.75
G-6	4
7	4.5
H-8	5
I-9	5.5
J-10	6
K-10½	6.5
L-11	8
M/N-13	9
N/P-15	10
P/Q	15
Q	16
S	19

CROCHET TERMINOLOGY

UNITED STATES		INTERNATIONAL
slip stitch (slip st)	=	single crochet (sc)
single crochet (sc)	=	double crochet (dc)
half double crochet (hdc)	=	half treble crochet (htr)
double crochet (dc)	=	treble crochet (tr)
treble crochet (tr)	=	double treble crochet (dtr)
double treble crochet (dtr)	=	triple treble crochet (ttr)
triple treble crochet (tr tr)	=	quadruple treble crochet (qtr)
skip	=	miss

■□□□ BEGINNER	Projects for first-time crocheters using basic stitches. Minimal shaping.
■■□□ EASY	Projects using yarn with basic stitches, repetitive stitch patterns, simple color changes, and simple shaping and finishing.
■■■□ INTERMEDIATE	Projects using a variety of techniques, such as basic lace patterns or color patterns, mid-level shaping and finishing.
■■■■ EXPERIENCED	Projects with intricate stitch patterns, techniques and dimension, such as non-repeating patterns, multi-color techniques, fine threads, small hooks, detailed shaping and refined finishing.

GAUGE

Exact gauge is **essential** for proper size. Before beginning your project, make the sample swatch given in the individual instructions in the yarn and hook specified. After completing the swatch, measure it, counting your stitches and rows carefully. If your swatch is larger or smaller than specified, **make another, changing hook size to get the correct gauge.** Keep trying until you find the size hook that will give you the specified gauge.

MARKERS

Markers are used to help distinguish the beginning of each round being worked. Place a 2" (5 cm) scrap piece of yarn before the first stitch of each round, moving marker after each round is complete.

JOINING WITH SC

When instructed to join with sc, begin with a slip knot on hook. Insert hook in stitch indicated, YO and pull up a loop, YO and draw through both loops on hook.

BACK RIDGE

Work only in loops indicated by arrows *(Fig. 1)*.

Fig. 1

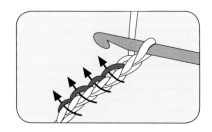

BACK OR FRONT LOOPS ONLY

Work only in loop(s) indicated by arrow *(Fig. 2)*.

Fig. 2

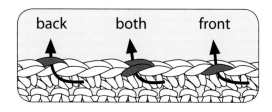

FREE LOOPS

After working in Back or Front Loops Only on a row or round, there will be a ridge of unused loops called the free loops. Later, when instructed to work in the free loops of the same row or round, work in these loops *(Fig. 3a)*.

When instructed to work in free loops of a chain, work in loop indicated by arrow *(Fig. 3b)*.

Fig. 3a   **Fig. 3b**

POST STITCH

Work around post of stitch indicated, inserting hook in direction of arrow *(Fig. 4)*.

Fig. 4

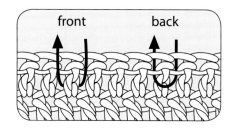

WORKING IN HORIZONTAL BAR

Work in bar indicated, inserting hook in direction of arrow *(Fig. 5)*.

Fig. 5

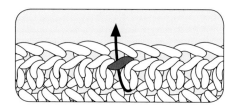

WEAVING SEAM

With **wrong** sides together, matching sts, and leaving an ample yarn end to weave in later, insert the needle from **back** to **front** under **both** loops of any sc on **both** pieces *(Fig. 6)*, then insert needle from **front** to **back** under **both** loops of next sc. Continue in this manner, drawing the seam together as you work.

Fig. 6

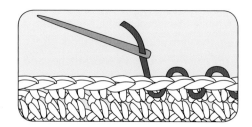

EMBROIDERY STITCHES
Backstitch

Backstitch is worked from **right** to **left**. Come up at 1, go down at 2 and come up at 3 *(Fig. 7)*. The second stitch is made by going down at 1 and coming up at 4.

Straight Stitch

Straight stitch is just what the name implies, a single, straight stitch. Come up at 1 and go down at 2 *(Fig. 8)*.

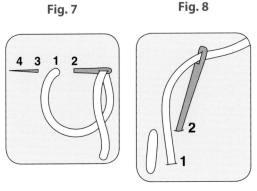

Fig. 7   **Fig. 8**

Satin Stitch

Satin stitch is a series of straight stitches worked side by side that touch but do not overlap *(Fig. 9a)* **or** come out of and go into the same stitch *(Fig. 9b)*. Come up at odd numbers and go down at even numbers.

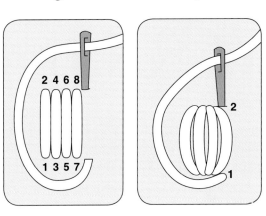

Fig. 9a   **Fig. 9**

Meet Kristi Simpson

Kristi Simpson enjoys designing cute baby gifts that mothers will love using. "There's just something special about having a handmade gift," she says. "It's personal and unique.

Inspired by her love of yarn, she creates crochet and knit patterns with a fresh and modern touch. The mother of five became hooked on crochet after teaching herself so she could help her daughter make a scarf from a "learn to crochet" kit that was a gift.

"I loved it from the beginning," she says. "I was amazed that I could take a string of yarn and create something so useful and pretty! Needless to say, I never stopped!"

Look for other Leisure Arts books featuring Kristi's designs at www.leisurearts.com/meet-the-designers/kristi-simpson.html. Visit kristisimpson.net or find her on Ravelry, Facebook, and Pinterest.

YARN INFORMATION

The Pillows in this book were made using Medium Weight Yarn. Any brand of Medium Weight Yarn may be used. It is best to refer to the yardage/meters when determining how many balls or skeins to purchase. Remember, to arrive at the finished size, it is the GAUGE/TENSION that is important, not the brand of yarn.

For your convenience, listed below are the specific yarns used to create our photography models. Because yarn manufacturers make frequent changes to their product lines, you may sometimes find it necessary to use a substitute yarn or to search for the discontinued product at alternate suppliers (locally or online).

BARRY BEAR
Lion Brand® Vanna's Choice®
Brown - #403 Barley
Red Heart® With Love®
Ecru - #1101 Eggshell

BETTY BUNNY
Red Heart® Soft®
White - #4600 White
Pink - #9273 Very Pink
Orange - #4422 Tangerine
Blue - #2515 Turquoise

ELLIS ELEPHANT
Red Heart® Baby Hugs™ Medium
Grey - #4410 Dolphin
Yellow - #4201 Sunny
White - #4001 Frosting
Blue - #4830 Pool

FIONA FISH
Red Heart® Soft®
Variegated - #9954 Bohemian
Pink - #9273 Very Pink
Grey - #9440 Light Grey Heather

FRANK FOX
Lion Brand® Vanna's Choice®
Rust - #135 Rust
White - #100 White
Black - #153 Black

GEORGE GIRAFFE
Red Heart® With Love®
Gold - #1207 Cornsilk
Brown - #1321 Chocolate

LARRY LION
Lion Brand® Vanna's Choice®
Tan - #305 Pearl Mist
Taupe - #125 Taupe
Blue - #105 Silver Blue

OLIVIA OWL
Red Heart® Baby Hugs™ Medium
Blue - #4820 Sky
Ecru - #4303 Shell
Pink - #4704 Happy
Light Pink - #4724 Pinkie
Peach - #4258 Peachie
Black - #4012 Ink

PENNY PENGUIN
Red Heart® Soft®
Black - #4614 Black
White - #4600 White
Orange - #4422 Tangerine

We have made every effort to ensure that these instructions are accurate and complete. We cannot, however, be responsible for human error, typographical mistakes, or variations in individual work.

Production Team: Instructional/Technical Editor - Lois J. Long; Graphic Artists - Kytanna McFarlin and Maddy Ross; Senior Graphic Artist - Lora Puls; Photo Stylist - Lori Wenger; and Photographer - Jason Masters.